Sticky Notes and Bible Quotes

Godly answers for sticky situations

LYRICS AND SCRIPT BY NAN ALLEN

MUSIC BY DENNIS ALLEN AND MARK ALLEN

ARRANGEMENTS BY DENNIS ALLEN

PRODUCED BY DENNIS AND NAN ALLEN

AVAILABLE PRODUCTS:

Choir Book 0-6330-8938-9

Listening CD 0-6330-8945-1
(available at a reduced rate when
bought in quantities of 10 or more.)

Listening Cassette 0-6330-8939-7
(available at a reduced rate when
bought in quantities of 10 or more.)

Accompaniment CD 0-6330-8941-9
(Split track and stereo tracks)

CD Promo Pak 0-6330-8942-7

Cassette Promo Pak 0-6330-8940-0

Bulletins 0-6330-8944-3

Posters 0-6330-8943-5

DOVETAIL MUSIC

Contents

The Word

NAN ALLEN

DENNIS ALLEN
Arranged by Dennis Allen

I'M NOTHING
SKETCH

*(Scene opens with **Leader** writing sticky notes and sticking them on a bulletin board, lunch boxes, notebooks, etc.) (NOTE: The Scripture verse may be read or recited by a child or several children.)*

Leader: Jeremy, don't forget your lunch. Hannah, soccer practice at 4:00 today. Sarah, good luck on your test. *(looks up and sees the audience)* Oh, hi. I'm just leaving some sticky notes. Great inventions, sticky notes. Just write a message and stick 'em on the refrigerator, the bulletin board, a notebook, any place you want to leave a reminder. Which reminds me that the Bible verses we learn are like, well, sticky notes on our brains. In Deuteronomy 6, God says this:

Child 1: "These commandments that I give you today are to be upon your hearts.

Child 2: "Impress them on your children. Talk about them when you sit at home and when you walk along the road, when you lie down and when you get up.

Child 3: "Tie them as symbols on your hands and bind them on your foreheads. Write them on the doorframes of your houses and on your gates."

Leader: Sounds like sticky notes to me. So, right now, we're gonna see some, well, sticky situations that we get ourselves into and how God's Word reminds us what to do.

*(**Josh**, wearing glasses, is sitting at the edge of the stage looking forlorn. **Leader** crosses to **Josh**.)*

Leader: What's the matter, Josh?

Josh: Nothing.

Leader: Something's the matter.

Josh: Nah, it's just that, well, I'm a total loser.

Leader: I'd say that's pretty tough language.

Josh: Yeah, well, it's true. I got cut from the baseball team today.

Leader: Ah, that's tough.

Josh: That's not all. My two best friends went on a camping trip and didn't invite me to go.

Leader: Oh…man…

Josh: I'm not finished. I tried out for the school play, and I got the part of a shrub.

Leader: A what?

Josh: A shrub. I couldn't even be a tree, something tall and straight. I'm a yard bush.

Leader: That's something.

Josh: That's nothing. There's not even a part for a shrub in the play. The teacher just felt sorry for me and added a shrub. *(mimicking the teacher)* Yeah, just stick some ol' leaves on ol' Josh and let him be a shrub. I'm nothing…nobody…a failure. Yeah, I'm flunking life if that's possible, and that's another thing. I flunked a math test today, too. What a loser!

Leader: Oh now, Josh. You know you're really special to God. In fact, you're a child of God.

Josh: Oh, please. If I'm His child, why didn't He give me two good eyes, not "four-eyes." Oh yeah, that's another thing.

Leader: *(to the choir)* Okay, guys. What do we need here?

Choir: A sticky note?

Leader: Yeah, with…

Choir: …a Bible quote.

Sticky Note No. 1

(recited over music)

"We are God's workmanship, created in Christ Jesus to do good works, which God prepared in advance for us to do" *(Ephesians 2:10).*

"I praise you because I am fearfully and wonderfully made" *(Psalm 139:14).*

"To all who received him, to those who believed in his name, he gave the right to become children of God" *(John 1:12).*

"Now if we are children, then we are heirs—heirs of God and co-heirs with Christ" *(Romans 8:17).*

Music by DENNIS ALLEN
Arranged by Dennis Allen

Children of God

NAN ALLEN

DENNIS ALLEN
Arranged by Dennis Allen

14

16

ME AFRAID?
SKETCH

(Scene opens as **Fearless** *[probably a boy] steps forward, acting very brave.)*

Fearless: I'm not afraid of anything!

Friend 1:   *(crossing to* **Fearless***)* Not anything?

Fearless: *(backing down a little)* Well, not much.

Friend 1:   What does "not much" mean?

Fearless: It means, well, I'm afraid of some things…I guess.

Friend 2:   *(crossing to* **Fearless***)* Like what?

(The following characters turn toward the audience. As they deliver their lines, **Fearless** *gets more and more scared, maybe putting his head down or covering his eyes, as if having these voices as visions.)*

Bully: *(clinching his fist and looking tough)* Okay, give me your lunch money or I'll give you a knuckle sandwich.

Friend 2:   *(looking nervous)* There was a drive-by shooting in the neighborhood last night.

Friend 3:   *(looking scared)* Did you hear about the bomb threat at the stadium?

Friend 4:   *(very scared)* It's a new virus. It eats your skin and then your eyeballs.

Fearless: Okay, okay. I'm afraid! So what do I do?

Leader: So glad you asked!

Sticky Note No. 2
(recited over music)

"The Lord is near to all who call on him, to all who call on him in truth" (Psalm 145:18).

"For he will command his angels concerning you to guard you in all your ways" (Psalm 91:11).

"The Lord your God goes with you; he will never leave you nor forsake you" (Deuteronomy 31:6).

"Do not let your hearts be troubled and do not be afraid" (John 14:27).

Music by MARK ALLEN
Arranged by Dennis Allen

(repeat as needed)

God Is Near

NAN ALLEN

MARK ALLEN
Arranged by Dennis Allen

Let not your heart___ be trou - bled, do not be a - fraid.___

Call on the Lord___ in truth,___

He will give you peace.___

WEAK DAYS

SKETCH

*(Scene opens as **Actor 1** steps forward holding a book. Looking at it, he or she snaps the book closed.)*

Actor 1:   I can't do it! I just can't do it! I give up.

*(**Actor 2** steps forward with a pencil and paper, then throws them down in frustration.)*

Actor 2:   It's too big a job! I'll never finish.

*(**Actor 3** steps forward, folding his or her arms in front.)*

Actor 3:   How can I do this? I don't even know where to start.

Leader: Need some help?

Actor 1:   Yes!

Actor 2:   Definitely!

Actor 3:   Please!

Leader: Okay, God's got a sticky note for this sticky situation.

Sticky Note No. 3
(recited over music)

"Finally, be strong in the Lord and in his mighty power" *(Ephesians 6:10).*

"We are weak, but you are strong" *(I Corinthians 4:10).*

"For nothing is impossible with God" *(Luke 1:37).*

"I can do all things through him who gives me strength" *(Philippians 4:13).*

"He who began a good work in you will carry in on to completion until the day of Christ Jesus" *(Philippians 1:6).*

Music by DENNIS ALLEN
Arranged by Dennis Allen

(repeat as needed)

15   *Celtic feel, in two* (♩. = ca. 66)

mp

Be Strong

NAN ALLEN

DENNIS ALLEN
Arranged by Dennis Allen

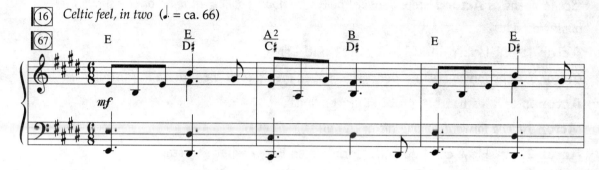

I WANT
SKETCH

*(Scene opens with **Girl 1** stepping forward holding a shoe box.)*

Girl 1:   I'll just die if I don't get these shoes.

Girl 2:   *(stepping forward with lots of jewelry)* Can a girl have too much jewelry?

Boy 1:   *(boy stepping forward)* PlayStation® 2! Saw it! Want it! Gotta have it!

Leader: I think somebody needs a…

Choir: …sticky note with a Bible quote!

Leader: Very good!

Sticky Note No. 4
(recited over music)

"Do not store up for yourselves treasures on earth, where moth and rust destroy, and where thieves break in and steal. But store up for yourselves treasures in heaven, where moth and rust do not destroy, and where thieves do not break in and steal. For where your treasure is, there your heart will be also" *(Matthew 6:19-21).*

Music by DENNIS ALLEN
Arranged by Dennis Allen

21   *Driving 60's (♩ = ca. 126)*   *(repeat as needed)*

Treasures

NAN ALLEN

DENNIS ALLEN
Arranged by Dennis Allen

THE GOOD, THE BAD, THE TEMPTED
SKETCH

*(Scene opens as **Tempted** steps forward, possibly sitting on a stool or on the edge of the stage. He sits as if trying to decide whether to do something. **Bad** and **Good** stand on either side of **Tempted** trying to persuade him.)*

Bad: Go ahead, do it.

Good: Don't do it. It's wrong.

Bad: Nobody'll know.

Good: You'll know. And God will know.

Bad: But you won't get in trouble.

Good: It doesn't matter. Wrong is wrong.

Bad: You're not going to listen to that voice, are you?

Good: You're not going to listen to that voice, are you? Do right!

Bad: Go ahead.

Good: Do right!

Bad: Do wrong.

Good: Do right!

Bad: Do wrong…

Tempted: Wait! Stop! Somebody help quick! Sticky note with a Bible quote, please!

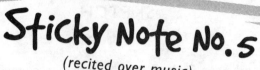

Sticky Note No. 5

(recited over music)

"Be self-controlled and alert. Your enemy the devil prowls around like a roaring lion looking for someone to devour" *(1 Peter 5:8).*

"Resist him, standing firm in the faith" *(1 Peter 5:9).*

"Put on the full armor of God so that you can take your stand against the devil's schemes" *(Ephesians 6:11).*

"Submit yourselves, then, to God. Resist the devil, and he will flee from you" *(James 4:7).*

"Greater is he that is in you than he that is in the world" *(1 John 4:4).*

Music by DENNIS ALLEN
Arranged by Dennis Allen

26 *With motion* (♩ = ca. 100)

(repeat as needed)

Resist Him

NAN ALLEN

DENNIS ALLEN
Arranged by Dennis Allen

45

NOT LIKE ME
SKETCH

*(**Actor 1** and **Actor 2** step forward and speak to each other.)*

Actor 1:   He doesn't look like me.

Actor 2:   She doesn't sound like me.

Actor 1:   He's weird.

Actor 2:   She's strange.

Actor 1:   I don't like him.

Actor 2:   I don't like her.

Actor 1:   That's okay. He doesn't like me either.

Actor 2:   Yeah, and she totally ignores me.

Leader: What do you say, guys? Does the Bible have something to say about loving people who are different or who don't like us?

Chior: Sticky note with a Bible quote!

Sticky Note No. 6
(recited over music)

"'Love the Lord your God with all your heart and with all your soul and with all your mind and with all your strength.' The second is this: 'Love your neighbor as yourself.' There is no commandment greater than these" *(Mark 12:30-31).*

"If you love those who love you, what reward will you get?" *(Matthew 5:46).*

"A new command I give you: Love one another. As I have loved you, so you must love one another" *(John 13:34).*

Music by MARK ALLEN
Arranged by Dennis Allen

(repeat as needed)

[32] *With motion* (♩ = ca. 86)

Love One Another

NAN ALLEN

MARK ALLEN
Arranged by Dennis Allen

52

WISH I HADN'T
SKETCH

*(Scene opens as **Actor 1** is trying to turn back the hands of a clock.)*

Actor 2: *(crossing to **Actor 1**)* So what are you doing with that clock?

Actor 1: Turning back time.

Actor 2: Why do you want to turn back time?

Actor 1: Maybe it'll undo what I did.

Actor 2: Oh, I see. You did something bad, huh?

Actor 1: Yeah.

Actor 2: And you think that turning a clock back would undo what you did?

Actor 1: Nah. But I don't know what else to do.

Actor 2: I have a suggestion.

Actor 1: Sticky note?

Actor 2: Yeah.

Sticky Note No. 7
(recited over music)

"If we confess our sins, he is faithful and just and will forgive us our sins and purify us from all unrighteousness" (1 John 1:9).

"Let us then approach the throne of grace with confidence, so that we may receive mercy and find grace to help us in our time of need" (Hebrews 4:16).

"Humble yourselves before the Lord, and he will lift you up" (James 4:10).

Music by MARK ALLEN
Arranged by Dennis Allen

Humble Yourselves Before the Lord

NAN ALLEN

MARK ALLEN
Arranged by Dennis Allen

FORGIVEN, FORGOTTEN
SKETCH

*(Scene opens as **Unforgiving** steps forward with a long paper list.)*

Unforgiving: See this list? I just finished it.

Actor 1: What's it a list of?

Unforgiving: It's a list of all the things that a certain person has done to me. I'm thinking about mailing it to the person. What do you think?

Actor 1: I don't think so.

Unforgiving: Okay, then maybe I'll put it in the newspaper so everybody else can see it, too.

Actor 1: Not a good idea.

Unforgiving: At least I'll put it up on my bulletin board.

Actor 1: No!

Unforgiving: Then what do I do with it?

Actor 1: Tear it up.

Unforgiving: What? Tear it up? No, I just made it.

Actor 1: Then put a sticky note on it.

Unforgiving: Sticky note? What would it say?

Sticky Note No. 8

(recited over music)

"Be kind and compassionate to one another, forgiving each other, just as in Christ God forgave you" *(Ephesians 4:32).*

"Love your enemies and pray for those who persecute you" *(Matthew 5:44).*

"God demonstrates his own love for us in this: while we were still sinners, Christ died for us" *(Romans 5:8).*

Music by DENNIS ALLEN
Arranged by Dennis Allen

forgiven

NAN ALLEN

DENNIS ALLEN
Arranged by Dennis Allen

WHAT To Do
SKETCH

*(Scene opens with **Actor 1** holding a "fortune-telling" toy.)*

Actor 1:   Come on. Should I do this? *(shakes the toy, looking at results)* Most definitely. Good. *(shakes the toy again)* Just to be sure. Should I do this? *(looking at results)* No. *(frustrated, shakes toy again)* Should I do this? *(looking at results)* Ask later. *(continues silently as **Actor 2** speaks)*

*(**Actor 2** steps forward, flipping a coin)*

Actor 2:   Heads, I do it. Tails, I don't. *(flips a coin, looks at it)* Best two out of three. *(flips a coin, looks at it)* Best three out of five.

*(**Actor 3** and **Actor 4** steps forward)*

Actor 3:   Rock, Paper, Scissors?

Actor 4:   Sure.

*(**Actor 3** and **Actor 4** play the game "Rock, Paper, Scissors")*

*(all continue silently as **Leader** speaks)*

Leader: Here's the right way to make a decision. You don't need a toy, a coin, or a game. This Bible quote is the best reminder.

Sticky Note No. 9
(recited over music)

"Trust in the Lord with all your heart and lean not on your own understanding; in all your ways acknowledge him and he will make your paths straight" *(Proverbs 3:5-6).*

"If any of you lacks wisdom, he should ask God, who gives generously to all without finding fault, and it will be given to him" *(James 1:5).*

"Lead me, O Lord, in your righteousness because of my enemies—make straight your way before me" *(Psalm 5:8).*

Music by DENNIS ALLEN
Arranged by Dennis Allen

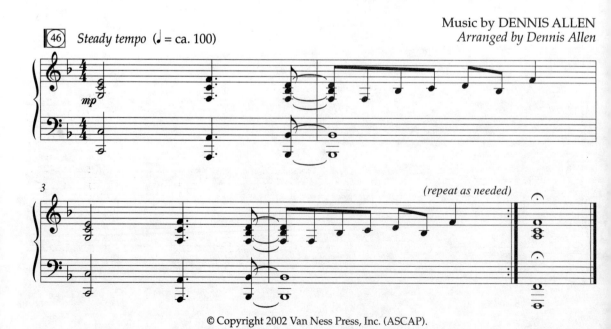

Lead Me, Lord

NAN ALLEN

DENNIS ALLEN
Arranged by Dennis Allen

STICKY NOTE ME

SKETCH

Leader: Yep, great invention a sticky note. With one of these you can leave a message like "I love you," "Have a great day!" or it can be used as a reminder to do something. "Don't forget your keys." "Doctor's appointment today at 2:00." A Bible verse you've memorized, whether it's in a song or not, is God's message to you and a reminder that He's there and that He has your best interest at heart.

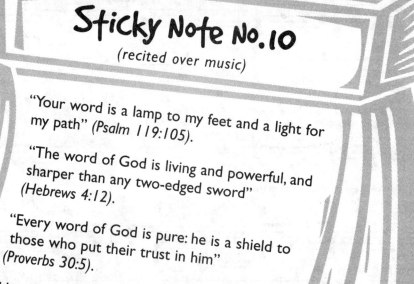

Sticky Note No. 10
(recited over music)

"Your word is a lamp to my feet and a light for my path" *(Psalm 119:105)*.

"The word of God is living and powerful, and sharper than any two-edged sword" *(Hebrews 4:12)*.

"Every word of God is pure: he is a shield to those who put their trust in him" *(Proverbs 30:5)*.

"Heaven and earth will pass away, but my words will never pass away" *(Mark 13:31)*.

"The word of the Lord is right and true; he is faithful in all he does" *(Psalm 33:4)*.

Music by DENNIS ALLEN
Arranged by Dennis Allen

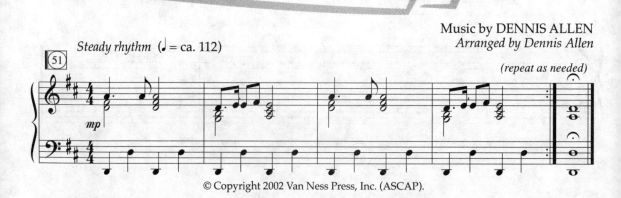

The Word
(Reprise)

NAN ALLEN

DENNIS ALLEN
Arranged by Dennis Allen

The Word, the Word, the Word is____ a lamp. The Word is____ a lamp to____ my feet. The Word, the Word, the Word is____ a light, a light un-to____ my path.

1. It is per-fect,____ sure,____ it's
2. It has al-ways____ been,____ will

3rd time to Coda

1st 2nd 3rd

2 3 4
56 57 58

PRODUCTION IDEAS

SET

At downstage right, the Leader may have a small table, a bulletin board and a stool. The table may hold lunch boxes, notebooks, etc. anywhere a sticky note may be left.

PROPS

Ball and glove; glasses *(for Josh in "I'm Nothing")*
Textbook *(for Actor 1 in "Weak Days")*
Pencil and paper *(for Actor 2 in "Weak Days")*
Shoe box *(for Girl 1 in "I Want")*
Jewelry *(for Girl 2 in "I Want")*
Stool *(for Tempted in "The Good, The Bad, The Tempted")*
Large clock with moveable hands *(for Actor 1 in "Wish I Hadn't")*
Long paper list *(for Unforgiving in "Forgiven, Forgotten")*
Fortune-telling toy *(for Actor 1 in "What to Do")*
Coin *(for Actor 2 in "What to Do")*

STAGING

Using the multimedia provided on the listening CD will enhance the performance. Detailed instructions and lyric sheets are included in a file on the CD. The cue sheets will give directions as to when to advance to the next shot on the screen.

Another idea is to take pictures of the children in the situations they set up in the sketches and then superimpose the sticky notes over the picture.

Other ideas could include taking slightly enlarged versions of sticky notes and sticking them on a large bulletin board or even on a person. Notes could be placed on the head, the chest, the hands, the arms, the face of the characters in the sketches.